The
World War II
Memorial

Tamara L. Britton
ABDO Publishing Company

visit us at
www.abdopub.com

Published by ABDO Publishing Company, 4940 Viking Drive, Edina, Minnesota 55435.
Copyright © 2005 by Abdo Consulting Group, Inc. International copyrights reserved in
all countries. No part of this book may be reproduced in any form without written
permission from the publisher. The Checkerboard Library™ is a trademark and logo of
ABDO Publishing Company.

Printed in the United States.

Cover Photo: Corbis
Interior Photos: Corbis pp. 16, 17, 18, 19; Getty Images pp. 5, 8, 9, 10, 13, 15, 20, 21,
    22, 23, 24, 25, 26, 27, 28, 29; Richard Latoff pp. 1, 6-7

Series Coordinator: Heidi M. Dahmes
Editors: Heidi M. Dahmes, Megan M. Gunderson, Megan Murphy
Art Direction & Maps: Neil Klinepier

Library of Congress Cataloging-in-Publication Data

Britton, Tamara L., 1963-
    World War II Memorial / Tamara L. Britton.
        p. cm. -- (Symbols, landmarks, and monuments)
    Includes index.
    ISBN 1-59197-837-8
    1. World War II Memorial (Washington, D.C.)--Juvenile literature. 2. World War,
1939-1945--Juvenile literature. I. Title: World War Two Memorial. II. Title: World
War 2 Memorial. III. Title.

D836.W37B75 2005
940.54'65753--dc22
                                                                    2004059458

Contents

National Memorial

In 1939, Germany invaded Poland. This started World War II. The United States entered the war in 1941. In the years that followed, international forces battled all over the world. They fought for freedom for the people of occupied nations.

Millions of American men and women answered the call of duty. Many **enlisted** in the armed forces. Those who stayed home also made many sacrifices. These contributions to the war effort assured unity in the quest for victory.

The National World War II Memorial is a symbol that honors all who served in the war. It also remembers those Americans who supported the troops from the home front. The monument acknowledges the efforts of a nation to achieve victory over **tyranny**.

The National World War II Memorial in Washington, D.C.

Fast Facts

√ The Battle of Normandy was fought in 1944. On June 6, 5,000 ships carried troops and weapons across the English Channel. Another 5,000 ships landed on the beaches of Normandy. It was the largest operation in history to use amphibious carriers for invasion.

√ Roger Durbin, a World War II combat veteran, attended a public meeting in Washington, D.C., in February 1987. There, Durbin asked Congresswoman Marcy Kaptur why a World War II memorial did not exist in the nation's capital. This was the first step in the 17-year process to establish a World War II monument.

√ The National World War II Memorial is located on the centerline of the National Mall. There was a lot of discussion as to whether the monument deserved such a revered spot.

√ The memorial is 384 feet (117 m) long and 279 feet (85 m) wide.

Timeline

1918   √   World War I ended.

1933   √   Adolf Hitler was named chancellor of Germany. Once in power, he turned the country into a dictatorship.

1939   √   On September 1, Germany invaded Poland. This marked the beginning of World War II.

1941   √   On December 7, Japan attacked Pearl Harbor, Hawaii; the next day, the United States officially joined the war.

1945   √   Japan surrendered to the Allies on September 2. World War II was over.

1987   √   Congresswoman Marcy Kaptur proposed her first bill for a memorial to commemorate all who served in World War II.

1993   √   On May 25, President Bill Clinton signed a bill authorizing the construction of the National World War II Memorial in Washington, D.C.

1995   √   The National World War II Memorial site was dedicated on Veterans Day.

2000   √   On Veterans Day, a ground-breaking ceremony was held.

2004   √   Construction of the memorial was completed; on April 29, the National World War II Memorial was opened to the public; a dedication ceremony was held May 29.

Between Wars

World War II officially began in 1939. But, its roots go back to the First World War. In 1918, **World War I** ended. Germany and its **allies** had lost. Leaders from the winning nations wrote the Treaty of Versailles.

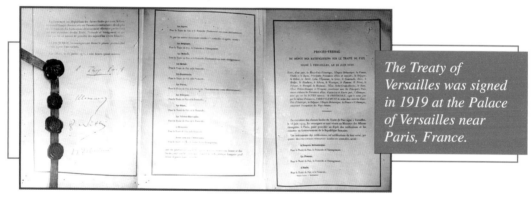

The Treaty of Versailles was signed in 1919 at the Palace of Versailles near Paris, France.

The treaty was harsh on Germany. The country had to give up land it had taken during the war. It also had to pay billions of dollars to the countries it had attacked. And, it could no longer have an army or navy. These terms weakened Germany's **economy**. It could not pay its huge war **debts**.

Germans take apart war machines outside Berlin. Under the Treaty of Versailles, Germany was required to disarm.

In addition to its **economy**, Germany's government was weakened, too. The German people were unhappy about losing the war. They felt the terms of the treaty were too severe. In the years after the war, many efforts were made to establish a new German government.

Adolf Hitler had fought in the war. He also thought the Germans were mistreated. He wanted to abolish the treaty and rebuild the nation. So, he took over the German Workers' Party and renamed it the Nazi Party. And, he began forming plans to make Germany powerful again.

In 1933, Hitler became Germany's **chancellor**. Once in power, he established himself as a **dictator**. He suspended

Adolf Hitler (left) *and Benito Mussolini*

the nation's **constitution** and declared **martial law**. He also began rebuilding the nation's armed forces. He wanted to recover the land Germany had lost in the Treaty of Versailles.

Hitler soon had help. Benito Mussolini had come to power in Italy. Mussolini had many of the same ideas as Hitler. So, Hitler saw Italy as an **ally**. In 1936, Germany and Italy formed the Rome-Berlin Axis. Japan eventually joined them. These countries became known as the Axis powers.

In 1938, French **premier** Édouard Daladier, British prime minister Neville Chamberlain, and Mussolini met with Hitler. They all signed the Munich Pact. The pact gave Hitler land in Czechoslovakia if he agreed to stop invading other countries.

But, the pact did not last. In March 1939, Hitler overtook Prague, the capital of Czechoslovakia. Then on September 1, 1939, Germany invaded Poland. Two days later, Great Britain and France declared war on Germany. Together with Russia, they formed the Allied powers. World War II had begun.

A Global Conflict

The first two years of the war did not go well for the **Allies**. The Axis powers invaded Norway and Denmark. In 1940, Italy joined the war on Germany's side and attacked France. On June 21, France surrendered. Next, Germany attacked the Soviet Union and began bombing England.

When the war began, the United States was a **neutral** country. Since **World War I**, Americans had maintained a policy of **isolationism**. They did not want to enter another European war. But Great Britain was an ally. Americans felt they should help.

The United States gave Britain ships and war supplies. This way, America could help its ally and still remain neutral. However, the United States also began to re-arm itself. This proved to be a smart idea. The United States would soon have no choice but to enter the war.

On December 7, 1941, Japan attacked the U.S. naval base at Pearl Harbor, Hawaii. The next day, the United States declared war against Japan. Three days later, Germany and Italy declared war on the United States. The world was again at war.

During the attack on Pearl Harbor, 19 ships were damaged or sunk, and more than 2,000 people were killed.

War in the Pacific

The Japanese continued to attack the United States in the Pacific. They invaded and occupied most of Southeast Asia. Japan also attacked the British territory of Hong Kong. In May 1942, the Philippines surrendered to Japan.

The United States went into action to recover land in the Pacific from Japan. On June 4, Japan attacked the Midway Islands. But, American forces defeated the Japanese. This ended Japan's expansion in the Pacific.

Energized by the victory at Midway, the **Allies** moved to take control. By January 1943, British forces defeated the Germans and Italians at El Alamein in the eastern Sahara. On May 12, the Axis armies were forced out of North Africa.

Allied troops moved toward Italy. They landed on the island of Sicily in July. Mussolini was removed from office and imprisoned. By June 5, 1944, Rome was freed from German control.

All but one of these pilots from an American navy torpedo bomber were killed during the attack on Midway.

On June 6, American, British, and Canadian troops landed on the beaches of Normandy, France. On August 25, Paris was liberated from the Germans. Next, **Allied** troops moved into Germany.

Back Home

America's military forces were fighting all over the world. But, the troops were not alone. At home, the American people were united with their military. They, too, were fighting to defeat the Axis powers and win the war.

The United States needed money to keep fighting. So, Americans bought millions of dollars worth of war **bonds**. This money went to the government to pay for the war. But most important, men who met the military's qualifications **enlisted** to keep the armed forces strong.

At that time, most women did not work outside the home. When the men left for war, more workers were needed to keep production going. So, women entered the

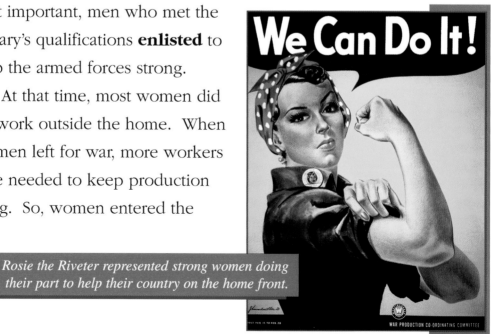

Rosie the Riveter represented strong women doing their part to help their country on the home front.

workforce. They built airplanes and made **ammunition**. Women produced goods needed both at home and abroad.

Americans also sacrificed food and other necessities during the war. Sugar, butter, gasoline, coffee, and meat were rationed. Shoppers could only buy a certain amount at one time. Americans made up for food shortages by growing their own food. This way, more food could be shipped to the soldiers. By their sacrifices, Americans showed their efforts to support the war any way they could.

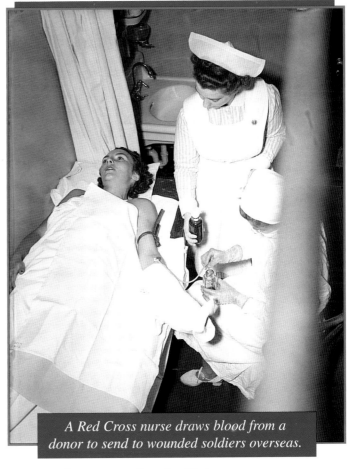

A Red Cross nurse draws blood from a donor to send to wounded soldiers overseas.

Victory

Back in Europe, the Axis powers were losing ground. Mussolini was killed trying to escape Italy. On April 30, 1945, Hitler killed himself. On May 4, Germany surrendered. Four days later, the **Allied** powers declared victory in Europe.

Fighting in Europe had ended, but the battle in the Pacific continued. American troops had been bombing Japan since 1943. In 1945, they began bombing Japan's major cities. But, the Japanese continued to fight.

President Harry S. Truman

President Harry S. Truman wanted to end the war. Many countries were in ruins, and millions of people had died. So, the president made a hard decision that had never been made before.

On August 6, 1945, the United States dropped an **atomic bomb** on the Japanese city of Hiroshima. Three days later, the United States bombed Nagasaki. The destruction from the bombs was overwhelming.

Japan's leaders realized they could not win against a weapon as powerful as the **atomic bomb**. So on September 2, 1945, Japan surrendered. World War II was finally over, and the **Allies** had won.

Truman (far right) displays the Japanese surrender document on September 7, 1945.

Honoring Veterans

Millions of men and women served in the war to defeat the Axis powers. They fought to protect freedom around the world. Many who went to war did not come home.

Congresswoman Marcy Kaptur

As the years passed, many Americans thought a national memorial for World War II **veterans** should be established. In 1987, 1989, and 1991, U.S. representative Marcy Kaptur proposed bills to build a memorial. But they did not pass.

Then in 1993, Congress finally passed a bill to authorize a World War II memorial in Washington, D.C. On May 25, President Bill Clinton signed Public Law 103-32.

The law authorized the American Battle Monuments Commission (ABMC) to establish a memorial. It also authorized the president to appoint 12 people to serve on the Memorial Advisory Board (MAB). The MAB would assist the ABMC with organizing the monument.

In October of that same year, Congress passed a bill approving the memorial site. It would be built in the monuments area of the National Mall. The president signed the bill on October 25. Finally, a national memorial honoring World War II **veterans** would be a reality.

Before 2004, the only memorial in the U.S. capital commemorating World War II veterans was the Iwo Jima Memorial. But, it only recognizes the marines. No memorial honored everyone who served in the war, at home or abroad.

Design Competition

The ABMC chose the Rainbow Pool area for the site of the National World War II Memorial. The pool is on the

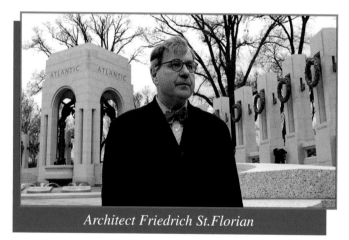

Architect Friedrich St.Florian

National Mall between the Lincoln Memorial and the Washington Monument. President Clinton **dedicated** the site on **Veterans** Day 1995.

Now the memorial had to be designed. In April 1996, the ABMC announced a design competition. **Architects** from all over the world submitted a total of 407 entries. From these, six were selected as finalists.

Friedrich St.Florian from Providence, Rhode Island, submitted the winning design. Other architects teamed up to assist him. George E. Hartman was the associate architect.

James van Sweden
was the landscape
architect. Ray
Kaskey would create
the memorial
sculptures.

St.Florian's initial
design was approved
in 1998. Final design
approval came on
September 21, 2000,
after some changes
were made.
Construction was set
to begin in
September 2001.

A view of the monument's placement on the National Mall.
The Lincoln Memorial is seen in the background.

Raising Money

Meanwhile, money had to be raised to pay for the memorial. In 1997, ABMC had created a fund-raising campaign. World War II **veterans** Senator Bob Dole and FedEx chief executive officer Frederick W. Smith were in charge of the campaign.

Senator Bob Dole

ABMC raised $195 million. Most of this money came from private contributions. And, the U.S. government gave $16 million to the project.

Leaders now had money, a building site, and a design. They were ready to begin. On Veterans Day 2000, a ground-breaking ceremony was held at the memorial site. On January 23, 2001, the National Park Service issued a construction permit. All the pieces were in place.

There were many objections to the start of construction on the monument. But, Congress passed a bill approving immediate construction. President George W. Bush signed the bill on Memorial Day 2001. Construction began that September.

Actor Tom Hanks and President George W. Bush at the dedication ceremony on May 29, 2004. Hanks was the spokesman for the memorial's fund-raising campaign.

A Visit to the Memorial

After three years of construction, the National World War II Memorial was complete. On April 29, 2004, the memorial opened to the public. A **dedication** ceremony was held on May 29.

A granite plaza surrounds the Rainbow Pool. As visitors enter the ceremonial entrance to the memorial, they pass two American flags. Here, 24 bronze bas-relief sculptures show scenes from the war at home and overseas.

Bas-relief sculptures are found near the entrance to the memorial. This kind of sculpture is cut so that the images project slightly from the surrounding surface.

From the entrance, visitors can see a ring of 56 granite pillars. These pillars are set in two semicircles around a central pavilion at each end of the monument. Each pillar holds two bronze wreaths. The wreaths symbolize America's contributions of strength and supplies to the war.

The two pavilions represent both regions where the war was fought. The North Memorial Pavilion represents the Atlantic region. The South Memorial Pavilion represents the Pacific area of the war. Both are 43 feet (13 m) tall. Inside each, four bald eagles hold a laurel that symbolizes victory.

The Freedom Wall stands at the west end of the memorial. There are 4,000 gold stars on the wall. Each star represents 100 **veterans** who died in the war.

Forever Remembered

Sixteen million Americans served in World War II. Of these, 670,000 were wounded and 405,000 died. The cost of the war in lives and money can never truly be known.

The Freedom Wall at the World War II Memorial

Those who benefited from the sacrifices of American soldiers were grateful. They wanted to express this gratitude. So, they built a monument to endure for many years. It will remind future generations of the war. And, it will forever honor those who worked together to defeat **tyranny**.

The National World War II Memorial honors the sacrifices of America's soldiers. It also recognizes the support of those at home who contributed to their victory. The memorial is a symbol of the commitment to freedom and liberty that Americans share with the world.

At the ceremonial entrance to the memorial, an announcement stone explains the purpose and location of the memorial:

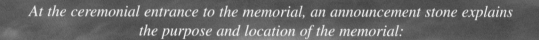

HERE IN THE PRESENCE OF WASHINGTON AND LINCOLN, ONE THE EIGHTEENTH CENTURY FATHER AND THE OTHER THE NINETEENTH CENTURY PRESERVER OF OUR NATION, WE HONOR THOSE TWENTIETH CENTURY AMERICANS WHO TOOK UP THE STRUGGLE DURING THE SECOND WORLD WAR AND MADE THE SACRIFICES TO PERPETUATE THE GIFT OUR FOREFATHERS ENTRUSTED TO US: A NATION CONCEIVED IN LIBERTY AND JUSTICE.

Glossary

allies - people or countries that agree to help each other in times of need.

ammunition - bullets, shells, and other items used in firearms.

architect - a person who plans and designs buildings. His or her work is called architecture.

atomic bomb - a bomb that uses the energy of atoms. It is thousands of times more powerful than a regular bomb.

bond - a certificate sold by a government. The certificate promises to pay its purchase price plus interest on or after a given future date.

chancellor - the chief minister of state in some European countries.

constitution - the laws that govern a country.

debt - something owed to someone, usually money.

dedication - a ceremony that officially sets aside something for a specific use.

dictator - a ruler with complete control who usually governs in a cruel or unfair way.

economy - the way a nation uses its money, goods, and natural resources.

enlist - to join the armed forces.

isolationism - the policy of a country that keeps it from getting involved in international affairs.

martial law - law administered by the military, when civilian enforcement agencies, such as police, can't maintain public order and safety.

neutral - not taking sides in a conflict.

premier - the highest-ranked member of some governments, also called a prime minister.

tyranny - cruel power used by a government.

veteran - a person who has served in the armed forces.

World War I - from 1914 to 1918, fought in Europe. Great Britain, France, Russia, the United States, and their allies were on one side. Germany, Austria-Hungary, and their allies were on the other side. The war began when Archduke Ferdinand of Austria was assassinated. The United States joined the war in 1917 because Germany began attacking ships that weren't involved in the war.

Web Sites

To learn more about the National World War II Memorial, visit ABDO Publishing Company on the World Wide Web at **www.abdopub.com**. Web sites about the World War II Memorial are featured on our Book Links page. These links are routinely monitored and updated to provide the most current information available.

Index